JN004187

Japanese Popular Culture in English

Discussions and Critical Thinking

日本のポップカルチャーで学ぶディスカッションと批判的思考

Robert Sheridan
Kathryn M. Tanaka
Jeanette M. Kobayashi

NAN'UN-DO

Cover art by Namiko N. Ookawara

Download Audio

音声ファイル
無料 DL
のご案内

このテキストの音声を無料で視聴（ストリーミング）・ダウンロードできます。自習用音声としてご活用ください。
以下のサイトにアクセスしてテキスト番号で検索してください。

https://nanun-do.com　テキスト番号［**512216**］

※ 無線 LAN（WiFi）に接続してのご利用を推奨いたします。

※ 音声ダウンロードは Zip ファイルでの提供になります。
お使いの機器によっては別途ソフトウェア（アプリケーション）の導入が必要となります。

※ Japanese Popular Culture in English: Discussions and Critical Thinking
音声ダウンロードページは以下の QR コードからもご利用になれます。

Read by

Guy Perryman（英）
Jennifer Skidmore（米）

Japanese Popular Culture in English: Discussions and Critical Thinking
Copyright© 2024

by
Robert Sheridan, Kathryn M. Tanaka, Jeanette M. Kobayashi

All Rights Reserved.
No part of this book may be reproduced in any form without written permission from the authors and Nan'un-do Co., Ltd.

Preface

We are delighted to share with you our textbook: *Japanese Popular Culture in English: Discussions and Critical Thinking*. We created it with careful consideration of the needs and interests of students studying in Japan as well as students who are curious about Japanese culture and its place in the world. In the following pages, we aim not only to improve your English skills but also to help you think more critically about Japanese contemporary culture and global society.

Popular culture is something that surrounds us every day. It is something we share with our friends and families. This textbook takes popular culture as a starting point to introduce topics for English discussion. After all, language learning is not just about speaking or reading. It is also about sharing culture. When you learn English, you may learn about different cultures through your language study, but you may also share Japanese culture with people living in other countries by using the English language.

We hope you will use this text as a way to think comparatively and critically about the different cultures you study. How do cultures relate to each other? What do we gain from thinking about global studies in Japan today? Keeping such questions in mind as you study will teach you something about yourself and your culture. Education can be an important journey, and we are excited to take it with you.

Finally, in conclusion, we need to thank many people. First of all, we would like to thank our expert authors, who contributed to this volume and believed in this project when it was just beginning. Their contributions inspired us and drove us to complete the textbook. Without them, and their hard work, this textbook would not have been possible. We would also like to thank the many students who have come before you and used the materials presented in this book before they were finalized. We are grateful for their engagement, feedback, and suggestions. Without the authors and our students, this book would not be in the form it is now. We know this book is better because of everyone who helped create it, and we give them our deepest thanks.

We hope that this textbook challenges you, helps you to develop some new perspectives, and is one of the first steps of your journey in cultural and global studies. We wish you the best of luck.

Robert, Kathryn, and Jeanette

Contents

Useful Expressions for English Conversations

Questions to Improve Comprehension

It is important to always ask questions when you do not understand something completely. Here are some questions that you could ask.

Could you say that again?	Could you please speak more slowly?
Could you please speak louder?	How do you spell that?
I'm sorry, but I don't understand.	What does this mean?
How do you say this in English/Japanese?	How do you say (pronounce) this word?

Rejoinders

We use rejoinders or short comments to show interest and to let the speaker know you are listening. Here are some rejoinders that you could use.

Happy	***Interested***
That's great!	I see.
Terrific!	That's nice.
Wonderful!	Oh, yeah?

Sad	***Surprised***
That's too bad.	You're kidding!
I'm sorry to hear that.	I can't believe it!
Oh, no!	Oh, really?!

Follow-up Questions

We use follow-up questions to talk more deeply about a topic. They are a great way to get more information and keep the conversation going. Here are some questions that you could ask.

Who (did/do) you _____ with?	Have you ever _____?
Where (did/do) you _____?	Which do you like better _____ or _____?
Why (did/do) you _____?	(Did/Do) you _____?
How often do you _____?	How (did/do) you get there?
When (did/do) _____?	How many/much _____ (did/do) you _____?
How long (did/do) you _____?	Can you _____?
What (did/do) _____?	What kind of _____ (did/do) you _____?

Expressing Opinions

We express our opinions to show we are listening and actively engaged in the topic. We also do it so we can learn from each other and this helps form our own opinions more clearly. Here are some ways that you could express your opinion.

Saying your opinion	*Agreeing*	*Disagreeing*
In my opinion, ...	I think so too.	I don't think so.
I think (that)...	That is a good point.	I'm not sure I agree.
I feel (that)...	That is true/right.	Maybe, but...
It seems to me (that)...	I agree.	I don't agree.

Asking for Other People's Opinions

We ask for other people's opinions when we want to learn new perspectives, or consider other ideas. Here are some ways that you can ask for someone else's opinion.

What do you think, (name)?	Do you agree, (name)?
What are your thoughts on this, (name)?	How do you feel about this, (name)?

Unit 1

The Eyes of Manga Characters

Activation activities: Pre-reading

a Give some examples of ways people communicate non-verbally (without speaking).

b Draw three faces expressing emotion and explain what they mean. Look at number **1.** as an example.

1.	2.	3.	4.

1. This person feels happy because they got a high score on their test.
2. ______________________________
3. ______________________________
4. ______________________________

c Trade worksheets with a partner. Look only at their pictures and write sentences to describe them below.

1. ______________________________
2. ______________________________
3. ______________________________

d Compare your descriptions with your partner's.

While-reading activities

a While reading the passage on the next page, list five words from the reading that you don't know. After you finish reading, check the meanings, and write an example sentence from a dictionary for each word so you can explain them to your classmates.

English word	Japanese meaning	Example sentence from the dictionary
Example: protagonist	主人公	The protagonist of my favorite manga is a pirate.
1.		
2.		
3.		
4.		
5.		

b In pairs or small groups, share your answers. Add any new words you learn from your classmates to the list below.

1.		
2.		
3.		

c Write a one-sentence summary of each paragraph. Look at number **1.** as an example.

1. Some people wonder why the eyes of manga characters are unnaturally large.
2. ______________________________
3. ______________________________
4. ______________________________

Reading

The Eyes of Manga Characters

Written by Yoshimi Kurata

DL 02

While I was doing a lecture and workshop on Japanese manga at an American college, one of the participants asked me: "Why do Japanese manga characters have large eyes? I ask because I think eyes are not that big." Indeed, one of the hallmarks of manga is the disproportionately large eyes of the characters. Sometimes they occupy half the face. I doubt any Japanese manga fans think about this as they read. As a reader, I never had. However, when I began to draw my own manga, I thought more about the size of the eyes and their significance.

So, why do manga characters have big eyes? Well, stories in manga are constructed to communicate emotion to the reader. While reading, the manga allows the reader to put themselves in the place of the protagonist or the main character. This sympathetically brings the reader into the world of the manga and should cause the reader to share the feelings of the protagonist. If the protagonist laughs, the reader laughs; and if the protagonist cries, the reader does as well. This feeling of sympathy is an important part of readers enjoying the story. Therefore, the artists must think not only about the words they use to tell the story but also about how the images add to the emotion they want to communicate to the reader.

There are set phrases or images that are often used to express emotions of anger and sadness when creating manga, and typically the story in the manga develops through rises and falls in emotion. But again, the manga artist expresses many of the emotions in the manga not through words, but with images. This is what communicates the feelings of the protagonist to the reader. And in this, the expression of the eyes carries the greatest weight.

There is a saying (*kotowaza*) that, "sometimes, the eyes speak much louder than the mouth ever could." If you look into the eyes of another person, you often know what they are trying to communicate without that person saying a word. If you look at the eyes, you can tell whether a person is happy, sad, furious, or overjoyed. In manga, I greatly exaggerate the eyes to make the emotions of my characters easier to understand. Moreover, just by looking at the eyes of the manga character, you can understand a great deal about the author of that manga. The eyes in manga are one of the important expressions of the personality of not only the characters but also of the manga artists.

Post-reading activities

1

a What is the saying (*kotowaza*) from the reading? Do you agree or disagree with it? Why?

b What are two more sayings (*kotowaza*) about communication?

Example The eyes are the window to the soul.（目は口ほどに物を言う）

1.

2.

c Interview two classmates and add their sayings about communication below.

1.

2.

d Choose two out of the four sayings above. Do you agree or disagree with them? Why?

2

a Think of other ways that we use body language in Japan to express nonverbal communication. In the table below, write the body part and how it is commonly used to express an emotion. Look at number **1.** as an example.

Body Part	How the body part is commonly used to express emotion
1. Eyebrows	We often raise our eyebrows to show we are interested in something or someone.
2.	
3.	
4.	

b Share your answers with a partner or in a small group. Listen to your partner(s) and add any new answers below.

Body Part	How the body part is commonly used to express emotion
1.	
2.	
3.	

c Body language can have different meanings in different countries. What do you think the following gestures mean? Compare your answers with the class.

Gesture	Country	Meaning
	America, UK:	"Everything is A-OK." This means everything is fine/great.
	France:	______________________________.
	Japan:	Money.
	America, UK:	Good work. Good luck.
	Iran, Greece:	______________________________.
	Japan:	______________________________.

d Do an internet search to try to find other examples of body language that can have different meanings in different countries.

Gesture	Country	Meaning

e Share your answers from **d** with a small group or partner.

Extension activities for The Eyes of Manga Characters

1 This article focused on the eyes in manga. Use the internet to research some other unique features of manga to show how the art or style is different from comic books. Summarize your findings in at least seven sentences to share with your classmates. Remember to cite your source.

OR

2 Pick a country other than Japan and research which Japanese manga is popular in that country. According to your research, why is it popular there? Summarize your findings in at least seven sentences to share with your classmates. Remember to cite your source.

Global Context

DL 03

Outside of Japan, French readers are the biggest consumers of manga. In fact, more than half of the comic books sold in France are manga! Beginning in the 1970s, anime and manga started to appear in France, and by 1978 the cartoon *Goldorak* (Japanese: *UFO Robot Grendizer*) was popular. This led French artists to partner with Japanese artists and create new series. French people love the creativity, humor, and freedom in manga such as the time-traveling Doraemon, and adventures that range from romance to fighting. Even French politicians admit to enjoying manga and anime like *Dragon Ball* or *One Piece*. French-themed manga like *Rose of Versailles* also has many fans. Today, France has a diverse manga market of Japanese and international artists, covering many genres. Manga popularity in France shows no signs of slowing.

Unit 2 Japanese Rituals and Food for the Gods

Activation activities: Pre-reading

a What is your favorite festival or holiday? Why?

b Draw pictures of three items associated with your favorite festival and explain what they mean. Look at number **1.** as an example.

1.	2.	3.	4.

1. Eating *Kuromame* or *black soybeans* during New Year's is a symbol of good health for the coming year.
2. ______________________________
3. ______________________________
4. ______________________________

c Do you think festivals are important? Why or why not?

d Share your answers from **a** – **c** with a small group or partner.

While-reading activities

a While reading the passage on the next page, list five words from the reading that you don't know. After you finish reading, check the meanings, and write an example sentence from a dictionary for each word so you can explain them to your classmates.

English word	Japanese meaning	Example sentence from the dictionary
Example: ritual	儀式	The kagura is a type of Shinto ritual dance.
1.		
2.		
3.		
4.		
5.		

b In pairs or small groups, share your answers. Add any new words you learn from your classmates to the list below.

1.		
2.		
3.		

c Look at the examples in box **A** and the grammatical expressions in box **B**:

A	B
• Carrots are known to be good for your eyesight. • Chocolate is supposed to help with depression.	________ represent(s) ________ ________ (be) supposed to ________ ________ (be) known to ________ ________ (be) thought to ________ ________ (be) a symbol of ________

Now list the various foods and rituals in paragraphs 1, 2, 3, and 4 write their importance using the grammatical expressions in box **B**.

Example The root vegetables are supposed to provide energy.

____

____

____

Reading

Japanese Rituals and Food for the Gods

Written by Carmen Săpunaru Tămaș

DL 04

In 1894, Professor Robertson Smith said that "food sharing is the classic, basic religious act among ancient and modern Near Eastern peoples." More than one hundred years later, we can say something similar about food sharing in Japan. In *Shinto*, the set of religious practices native to Japan, offering food to the gods is one of the most important gestures performed during the sacred ritual known as *Shinji*. A *Shinji* has four major parts: purification, a food offering, prayer, and *kagura*, the sacred dance. The food presented to the *kami* (gods) is called *shinsen*, and the basic components are water, salt, rice, and *sake*. They represent the fundamental food needs (water and rice), the connection with the sacred (salt for purification), and *sake* (as a luxurious drink).

Depending on the season, event, and area where the ritual occurs, other foods may be added to the list. For example, during *Tenjin Matsuri*, which is one of the three greatest festivals of Japan, boiled *mochi* rice with pickled plums (*umeboshi*) and root vegetables (*konsai*), gourds (*hyotan*), and cucumbers make up the meal for *Sugawara no Michizane*, the god *Tenjin*. The *mochi* rice is boiled at a high temperature to make it last longer in the Japanese summer heat. The traditional *Tenjin bento* (packed lunch) consisted of boiled rice and pickled plums (*umeboshi*), wrapped in bamboo bark, which is known to have antibacterial properties. The root vegetables are supposed to provide energy, while the cucumbers are thought to have a cooling effect. In a village in Miyazaki Prefecture, wild boars (*inoshishi*) hunted on the day of the festival are a gift for the gods. In Suwa, Nagano Prefecture, deer and rabbits are offered to the gods.

After being given to the *kami*, the *shinsen* is shared among the participants. Most Japanese festivals include a special meal called *naorai* where the people directly involved in the event eat together. *Naorai* is a sacred meal, where humans eat together with the gods, enjoying the short time when the gods are supposed to exist with the believers. All the important moments in a year have symbolic food. For example, the black beans (*kuromame*) eaten on New Year's Day are thought to bring health, while the fish eggs (*kazunoko*) are thought to bring the hope of having children. On *Hina Matsuri* (Girls'/Dolls' Festival), three-colored rice cakes (*hishimochi*) are eaten. The white of the cake represents snow and purity, the pink represents peach flowers that keep away evil, and the green is a symbol of the fresh spring plants that bring good health.

Japan is a country rich in sacred events and celebrations, and most of them are associated with a special food that has a symbolic meaning. This turns the simple act of eating into a ritual gesture. Eating these ritual foods represents a connection to tradition, history, and social practices which are a defining part of culture.

Post-reading activities

1

a Think of three comprehension questions based on the article to quiz your partner.

Example Q: Why do people eat root vegetables during *Tenjin Matsuri*?

1. ______________________________

2. ______________________________

3. ______________________________

b Ask your partner the three questions you wrote above. Work together to write down the correct answers below.

Example A: They are supposed to provide enegy.

1. ______________________________

2. ______________________________

3. ______________________________

c Think of two examples of *Shinto* rituals in your life. Describe them here.

____

____

____

____

____

____

d Share your answers with a partner. Do you have any ideas in common? If so, list them below. If not, write their new ideas below.

____

____

____

____

____

____

2 Using Key Phrases

______________	represent(s)	______________________________
______________	(be) supposed to	______________________________
______________	mean(s)	______________________________
______________	(be) known to	______________________________
______________	(be) thought to	______________________________
______________	(be) a symbol of	______________________________

a Using the expressions you learned above, write five sentences to describe a foreign or Japanese cultural festival or holiday.

Cultural festival or holiday: ______________________________

____

____

____

____

____

____

b Listen to two classmates describe the cultural festival or holiday they chose and summarize what you learned below.

____

____

____

____

____

____

Extension activities for Japanese Rituals and Food for the Gods

1 Pick a holiday or festival in a foreign country and research the food associated with it. What foods are served in rituals and what is their symbolism? Summarize your findings in at least seven sentences to share with your classmates. Remember to cite your source.

OR

2 Pick a Japanese holiday or festival and research its origins and how it has changed over time. What symbols are the same? What has changed? Summarize your findings in at least seven sentences to share with your classmates. Remember to cite your source.

Global Context

DL 05

Many of the foods we think of as everyday items today actually have origins in important rituals. Historically, food has had multiple uses such as practical, medicinal, and ritual. One great example of this is chocolate. For ancient people in Central America, cacao beans, from which chocolate is made, played an important part in many ritual events, including marriage and fertility. Marriage rituals included exchanging cocoa beans and with some of them, also exchanging cocoa drinks. When a baby was born, cacao seeds would be mixed with flowers for a ritual bath. From the case of chocolate, we can see the ritual and medicinal origins of a global food.

Unit 3

Animation in Japan

Activation activities: Pre-reading

a What is your favorite animation? Why?

b Which do you like better, Disney or Ghibli? Why?

c Give an example of a film with a social message. What is the message?

d Share your answers from **a** – **c** with a small group or partner.

While-reading activities

a While reading the passage on the next page, list five words from the reading that you don't know. After you finish reading, check the meanings of each word. Finally, find some of the different forms of the words (noun, verb, adjective, adverb). Be prepared to share them with your classmates.

English word	Japanese meaning	Different forms of the word
Example: reveal	明らかにする	(noun) revelation (adjective) revealing revelatory (verb) reveal (adverb) revealingly
1.		
2.		
3.		
4.		
5.		

b In pairs or small groups, share your answers. Add any new words you learn from your classmates to the list below.

1.		
2.		
3.		

c What is each paragraph in the article about? Look at number **1.** as an example.

1. **The influence of Walt Disney's work on anime.**
2. ______________________________
3. ______________________________
4. ______________________________
5. ______________________________

Animation in Japan

Written by Mark Schilling[1]

DL 06

The work of animation pioneer Walt Disney and his studio has had a huge influence on anime, Japan's contribution to animation. Tezuka Osamu has often been referred to as the "god of manga." He watched Disney's *Bambi* so many times that he knew every frame of the film by heart. And it was Tezuka who made Japan's first animated TV series, *Tetsuwan Atomu* (*Astro Boy*), in 1963. *Astro Boy* became a global hit on television, but Walt Disney made movie animation popular. How do Disney animations compare with Japanese anime today?

One of Japan's most famous animators, Hayao Miyazaki, considered Disney too simple and silly. He thought that the animation itself was great, but the stories did not properly show human feelings. Hayao Miyazaki wanted to make animated films that included foreign influences but also reflected his own tastes, interests, and concerns. He wanted to make films that appealed to both children and adults with high art standards films that also had realistic and identifiable emotions.

Miyazaki worked for a few anime studios before he started his own production company, Studio Ghibli, with another animator, Isao Takahata, and producer Toshio Suzuki. His films drew attention because they were strongly imagined, highly complex worlds that reflected present-day concerns. Many of his films won top film awards and became popular all over the world. For foreign fans, Miyazaki's animation and manga revealed new possibilities in forms many had thought were for children. His basic themes, such as peace, friendship, or the importance of nature, were familiar, but he used images in new and exciting ways that encouraged creative thought and imagination.

Miyazaki has become Japan's most successful commercial film producer, but he has always been very much an idealist and a social critic. In an interview for *Pacific Friend* magazine, Miyazaki said, "Japanese today have nothing to rely on in their minds. They have separated themselves from their own natural and spiritual environment. In my movies for children, I want to express...the idea that the world is a complicated and beautiful place. I want to tell them they are lucky to have entered into this world."

Critics and colleagues have great respect for Miyazaki's sense of fantasy and his ability to make films that audiences can believe in. Others like his ability to deal with complex social issues in children's films. Although he is in his eighties (he was born in 1941), Miyazaki continues to create animation and, through his art, comment on issues faced by both present-day Japan and the world beyond. Although he is not one of the first animators in Japan, he has changed the face of animation with his uniquely beautiful films.

[1] Based on the entry for "Hayao Miyazaki" in my book, *The Encyclopedia of Japanese Pop Culture, Boston,* MA: Weatherhill Press, 1997.

Post-reading activities: Individual

1 Write about your favorite Ghibli film. (If you do not have a favorite Ghibli film, write about your favorite animated film.)

a Using points from the article, describe the plot of your favorite film and what is important about the movie.

____

____

____

____

____

____

____

____

b Describe your favorite character(s) in the film. Why do you like them?

____

____

____

____

c Describe any social message in the film.

____

____

____

____

Post-reading activities: Interview 2 of your classmates

2 You are a reporter for a magazine about pop culture. Interview two classmates about their favorite Ghibli films. If they do not have a favorite Ghibli film, ask about their favorite animated film.

1. Name	
What is your favorite Ghibli film?	
What happens in the film?	
Who are your favorite characters in the film? Why?	
What are the social themes in the film?	

2. Name	
What is your favorite Ghibli film?	
What happens in the film?	
Who are your favorite characters in the film? Why?	
What are the social themes in the film?	

Extension activities for Animation in Japan

1 Although Hayao Miyazaki is the most famous animator in Japan today, there are many other popular anime films. Pick a smaller Japanese studio and research the kinds of films they make. What are their reasons for creating films? What are some of the features of their art style or themes in their films? Summarize your findings in at least seven sentences to share with your classmates. Remember to cite your source.

OR

2 Pick a Hayao Miyazaki film and watch it. Analyze the animation and discuss the big themes in the work. How does the art reflect the themes in the movie or ideas discussed in the article? Summarize your findings in at least seven sentences to share with your classmates. Remember to cite your source.

Global Context

DL 07

When people talk about animation, they often forget one kind of animated filmmaking called stop-motion animation. This is when objects are moved in very small steps and each step is individually photographed before putting the images together in a film. This technique dates back to the earliest days of cinema. Spanish filmmaker Segundo de Chomón used stop-motion animation in 1906 to create a stop-motion animation film, *Le théâtre de Bob*. Films such as *The Nightmare Before Christmas* (1993) and *Fantastic Mr. Fox* (2009) have kept stop-motion animation popular at a time when many studios are using digital techniques. Stop-motion animation is an important form of animation art that does not receive much attention; however, it is as old as cinema itself and continues to be an important part of North American and European animation.

Unit 4 Popular Fiction and Changing Ways of Reading

Activation activities: Pre-reading

a Who are some of your favorite authors? Write the names in the box below.

b If you want to learn more about your favorite authors, what can you do? Write the ways in the box below.

c What was reading like 30 years ago compared to today? Think about what kinds of things people read, and how they read. Write your ideas in the diagram below.

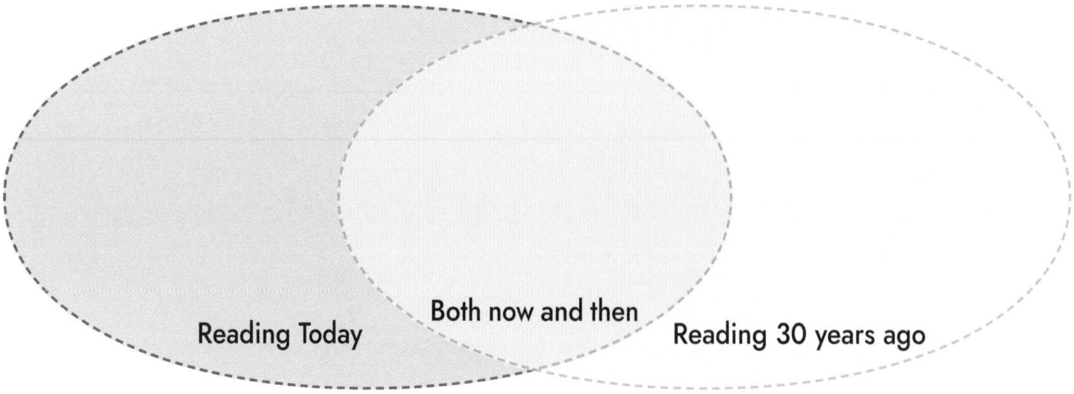

d Do you think literature is an important part of popular culture? Why or why not?

While-reading activities

a While reading the passage on the next page, list five words from the reading that you don't know. After you finish reading, check the meaning of each word. Finally, draw a picture of each word to help you remember it. Be prepared to share them with your classmates.

English word	Japanese meaning	A picture to help you remember the word	English word	Japanese meaning	A picture to help you remember the word
Example: interact	相互に作用する		3.		
1.			4.		
2.			5.		

b In pairs or small groups, share your answers. Add any new words you learn from your classmates to the list below.

1.			3.		
2.			4.		

c Write a one-sentence summary for each paragraph of the article. Look at number **1.** as an example.

1. **The way people read and communicate has been changed by technology in several important ways.**
2. ____________________
3. ____________________
4. ____________________
5. ____________________

Reading

Popular Fiction and Changing Ways of Reading

Written by Kathryn M. Tanaka

DL 08

In Japan, literature has been changed by new technologies. In fact, technology has changed the way people read and communicate in several important ways. According to literature scholar Alisa Freedman, technology means that for some popular authors in Japan, their writing style has changed. With the arrival of cell phone culture in the early 2000s, people began writing and reading novels on their smartphones. They began using simple, direct text messages and *emoji* to communicate. Some authors reflect a simpler style in their writing.

One modern author has driven a new kind of interest in Japanese literature at home and abroad. Haruki Murakami is a best-selling Japanese author whose work has been translated into more than 50 languages. He often writes in the first person, a style that has been described as simple. Similar to Murakami, authors such as Sayaka Murata and Mieko Kawakami have also become internationally popular, writing texts whose style seems simple but in them they deal with complex social issues.

However, technology has changed literature in another way. An important part of Murakami's popularity is the community his fans have created. He has run websites, radio shows, and newspaper columns where he interacts with his fans directly, sharing music, answering their questions, and giving advice. This creation of channels of direct communication with the audience is a new feature of literature in popular culture.

Authors now have Instagram, Facebook, or other SNS (social networking sites) where they interact with fans. Some famous authors now post things such as poems on SNS daily. For many authors, their SNS presence is bilingual. This encourages readers from abroad to take an interest in their works. Interactive fan communities are built around popular and aspiring authors as well. Writers interact with their fans and post very short works or extracts of longer work on social media. This interaction allows authors to receive instant feedback on their work. Literature is accessible in a way that it was not before SNS. Japanese authors have started using social media as a platform to connect with fans as well as develop new forms of literature.

Literature may seem an unlikely source of global popular culture, particularly in Japan. After all, the number of Japanese speakers outside Japan is quite low compared to English, Spanish, or Chinese speakers. However, authors who post their work on social media such as Murakami or Kawakami have greatly impacted global literature. Now, people can share their love of Japanese literature and find communities online.

Post-reading activities: Individual

a Write three open-ended discussion questions you have after reading the article.

Example If you were to write to your favorite author, what would you ask them?

1. ______________________________
2. ______________________________
3. ______________________________

Examples of open-ended discussion questions:
Why do you think...? How do you feel about...? Would you rather ... or ...? If you were..., what would you do? Have you ever...? What do you think is the best way to...?

b Write your answers to your three open-ended discussion questions above.

1. ______________________________
2. ______________________________
3. ______________________________

Post-reading activities: In pairs or a small group

1

a Ask a classmate your three discussion questions and write their answers in the table below.

b Do you agree or disagree with their opinion? Why? Explain to your partner why you agree or disagree.

a Name: Their answers:	b Do you agree or disagree with their opinion? Why? I (dis) agree because...
1.	
2.	
3.	

2 What kind of conversations do you think writers have with their fans on social media?

a In pairs or small groups, choose one of the following two activities and complete the task in the box below.

Activity 1 Create a conversation that you think writers may have with their fans on social media.

OR

Activity 2 Visit an author's blog or SNS page and write in English about an interesting post or conversation you find.

b
- If you did **activity 1**, insert *emoji* into the conversation you created in the box above.
- If you did **activity 2**, write your answer in the box below. Were any *emoji* used? If so, would you use the same ones? Why or why not? If no *emoji* were used, which ones would you use? Why?

c Share your answers from **a** and **b** with another partner or small group.

Extension activities for Popular Fiction and Changing Ways of Reading

1 Pick a famous contemporary author who posts on SNS. What kind of posts are they making? What kind of image do they present? How do they use their SNS to communicate with fans? Summarize your findings in at least seven sentences to share with your classmates. Remember to cite your source.

OR

2 Write a poem using emoji, short sentences, or other new ways of writing. Discuss your work: why did you pick the emoji? What meaning does it have to you? How is the emoji different from a word? Share your poem with classmates.

Global Context

DL 09

Emoji are important in modern life as they are used by about 90% of technology users. Early *emoji* were written in text but differed depending on the country. English and European languages used *emoji* that were horizontal :), whereas East Asian languages such as Japanese used vertical *emoji* (^_^). There are also other important cultural differences when interpreting the meaning of *emoji*. For example, the "horns" hand gesture (🤘) can show encouragement in some countries, but in countries such as Italy, it means your partner is cheating on you. A wave (👋) in China is a sign of cutting off a relationship, and in other cultures, it can be a sign of sexual intercourse. *Emoji* are not universal, so it is important to be aware of these cultural differences.

Unit 5 Japanese Cuisine Goes Global

Activation activities: Pre-reading

a Have you or someone you know ever tried Japanese food overseas? What did you/they think? Why?

b Do you think Japanese food is popular in foreign countries? Why or why not?

c Share your answers from a – b with a small group or partner.

d What do you consider authentic Japanese food? What do you consider non-authentic Japanese food? Brainstorm with a partner or small group.

Authentic Japanese food:	Non-authentic Japanese food:

While-reading activities

a While reading the passage on the next page, list five words from the reading that you don't know. After you finish reading, check the meanings, and write an example sentence from a dictionary for each word so you can explain them to your classmates.

English word	Japanese meaning	Example sentence from the dictionary
Example: entrepreneur	企業家	The entrepreneur started a new fashion business.
1.		
2.		
3.		
4.		
5.		

b In pairs or small groups, share your answers. Add any new words you learn from your classmates to the list below.

1.		
2.		
3.		

c In the table below, describe the three Japanese restaurants in Ireland discussed in the reading passage.

Name of Restaurant	Chef's name	Location	Additional Information
1.			
2.			
3.			

Reading

Japanese Cuisine Goes Global

Written by Rossella Ceccarini

DL 10

Have you ever eaten at a *Nanchatte Nihon Shokuten*? It is a restaurant outside of Japan claiming to be Japanese while serving a local version of Japanese food. For example, serving miso soup as a stand-alone dish, slices of cheese on top of *nigiri* sushi, or sushi pizza. And now, the Japanese government is trying to define genuine Japanese cuisine abroad. However, it is difficult to prove authenticity as the food changed to reflect local surroundings. Moreover, local versions of Japanese food have made their way back to Japan. The California Roll is a famous example. It was created in the 1960s by Japanese chefs living in the United States but is now also popular in Japan.

The globalization of Japanese food involves several groups of people such as Japanese settlers and migrants living overseas, tourists looking to make Japanese dishes they tried while in Japan, and chefs and entrepreneurs opening Japanese restaurants abroad. In the globalization of Japanese food, Ireland is an interesting example. The longest-running Japanese restaurant, Yamamori, was opened in the mid-1990s by Derek Ryan, an Irish entrepreneur who had been interested in Japanese cuisine. In addition to Yamamori's three restaurants as of 2023, you can also find more sushi and ramen chains, which usually belong to non-Japanese entrepreneurs. However, it's outside the capital city of Dublin where people might find true Japanese food.

Two Japanese restaurants in Ireland have received a Michelin star. The first was Shiro, located in the tiny village of Ahakista. A German-Japanese couple, Werner Pilz and his wife Kei, opened Shiro in their living room in the 1980s. When it first opened, it only had two tables. Werner served and entertained guests while Kei prepared the dishes and met the guests after the meal. Even though it started as a pastime, it achieved one Michelin star each year between 1996 and 2001.

The second restaurant to receive a Michelin star was Ichigo Ichie in Cork. It offers a traditional multi-course Japanese dinner known as *kaiseki*. It was opened in 2018 by Chef Takashi Miyazaki and was awarded a star in 2019 that was confirmed in 2020, 2022, and 2023. Chef Miyazaki moved to Ireland in 2008 with his Irish wife. Before opening Ichigo Ichie, Chef Miyazaki opened a small takeaway restaurant serving homemade Japanese food, also in Cork. After successfully introducing regional specialities such as *takoyaki*, *udon*, and *soba* to the community, Miyazaki opened a *kaiseki* restaurant to show that Japanese cuisine is more than sushi. His dishes are a mix of Japanese and Irish ingredients.

Japanese cuisine entered countries at different times, introduced by both Japanese and non-Japanese. Upon reaching a new country, Japanese cuisine adapted to the local context leading to the creation of new and popular recipes. The search for authenticity and the creation of dishes adapted to local tastes have equally contributed to the popularity of Japanese cuisine around the world.

Post-reading activities: Individual

a Think of three questions based on the article to quiz your partner.

Example Q: What was the first Japanese restaurant to get a Michelin star in Ireland?

1. ______________________________
2. ______________________________
3. ______________________________

b Ask your partner the three questions you wrote above. Work together to write down the correct answer below.

Example A: It was Shiro.

1. ______________________________
2. ______________________________
3. ______________________________

c Together with your partner, think of *three open-ended questions* based on the article. Then interview another person from your class and write down their answers to your questions.

Examples of open-ended questions:
Why do you think...? How do you feel about...? Would you rather ... or ...? If you were..., what would you do? Have you ever...? What do you think is the best way to...?

Open-ended Discussion Questions:	Name of a new partner: ______________ Answers:
1.	
2.	
3.	

d Use the language below to report your questions and answers from above to a different partner from your class.

I interviewed (student's name).
The first question I asked them was "..." They said that ...
The second question I asked them was "..." They told me that ...
The third question I asked them was "..." They thought that ...

Post-reading activities: Pairs/Small groups

a Choose a city in a foreign country and research the local food and popular dishes in that city. Then think of some Japanese dishes that might suit that local environment and explain why.

Name of city and country:	
Local food and popular dishes:	
Japanese food recommendations:	

b Share your answers with a person from a different pair/group. Listen to your new partner and write down their answers.

Name of city and country:	
Local food and popular dishes:	
Japanese food recommendations:	

Extension activities for Japanese Cuisine Goes Global

1 Pick a foreign country and research Japanese cuisine in that country. What kinds of restaurants seem to be available? What kind of Japanese food is the most popular? What are some examples of local adaptations of Japanese cuisine? Summarize your findings in at least seven sentences to share with your classmates. Remember to cite your source.

OR

2 Pick a foreign country and research local foods and cuisine. Then, design a Japanese dish that also uses these local foods. How do they complement each other? What would the dish look like, and how would it be cooked? How would it be served? Summarize your findings and ideas in at least seven sentences to share with your classmates. Remember to cite your source.

Global Context

DL 11

Globally, one of the most common sushi toppings is salmon, but to some people, there are some strange ones as well. For foreigners in Japan, things like *natto* and *shirako* may be strange and hard to eat. Outside of Japan, we can find tortilla sushi and donut sushi in different parts of North and South America. In Thailand, some chefs have even experimented with insect sushi. But more than that, other chefs are taking their foods and making sushi roll versions of them such as cheeseburger sushi, ice cream sushi, and waffle sushi. These foods are made to look like sushi but do not contain rice or fish. This begs the question, what makes a dish sushi at all? Is it the ingredients? The shape? As sushi becomes global cuisine, it becomes almost anything.

Unit 6

The Development of Relationships Between Humans and Animals

Activation activities: Pre-reading

a Have you ever kept a pet? Why or why not? Give at least two reasons.

b Give some examples of why people keep animals.

c Do you think the reasons for keeping animals have changed over time? Why or why not? Give at least two reasons.

d Share your answers from a – c with a small group or partner.

While-reading activities

a While reading the passage on the next page, list five words from the reading that you don't know. After you finish reading, check the meanings, and write an example sentence from a dictionary for each word so you can explain them to your classmates.

English word	Japanese meaning	Example sentence from the dictionary
Example: crops	作物	The farmer harvested the crops.
1.		
2.		
3.		
4.		
5.		

b In pairs or small groups, share your answers. Add any new words you learn from your classmates to the list below.

1.		
2.		
3.		

c Write a one-sentence summary of each paragraph. Look at number **1.** as an example.

1. **Relationships or bonds between humans and animals have changed to the point where it is now difficult for some people to keep a pet.**
2. ______________________________
____
3. ______________________________
____
4. ______________________________
____
5. ______________________________
____
6. ______________________________
____

Reading

The Development of Relationships Between Humans and Animals

Written by Yuka Nakajima

DL 12

The relationships between humans and pets have changed over time. Throughout history, animals and humans have assisted each other and formed strong relationships. However, the bond between them has become different with changes in society. This bond has strengthened, but this has made it difficult for some humans to commit to keeping a pet.

Animals have always been good workers for people. Dogs have helped with hunting, work around the home, and protecting their families. Cats have been kept to catch mice and protect crops. It was also beneficial for animals to live with humans as they no longer had to worry about food, the cold, or being attacked. Pets have been objects of people's love and attachment. People feel better from hugging dogs and cats. Animals have been the "pet" of people for more than 7000 years.

However, peoples' relationships with pets have greatly changed during the last 60 years, mainly in more developed countries such as Japan. Animals have turned from "pets" to "companions" or "family members." The change began during the 1980s. Before this time, it was common for people to find abandoned mixed-breed dogs or cats and keep them. However, a so-called "pet boom" happened during the economic bubble in the 1980s. People started to pay a lot to purchase purebred animals. After the 1980s, pets started living inside the house and became family members.

One reason to keep pets inside the home might have been because they were expensive. Another reason might be that they were cuter than mixed-breed dogs or cats. Purebred animals have been selected to match people's tastes. Research has shown that people feel more attached to animals with big eyes, round faces and figures, and whose facial features are centered. This set of features is called "baby schema," typically seen among mascot characters (*yuru-kyara*) in Japan. Living together inside also meant that pets started becoming important family members.

In recent years, this tendency has become stronger, but problems have arisen. With the declining birthrate, people care for animals as if they were their children. They try to give the best care when their pets get old. However, people suffer serious pet-loss syndrome when their pets die, and many do not want a pet again after such a loss. Moreover, some elderly people may need comfort, but they refuse to keep pets because they do not want to leave their "children" alone in this world after their death.

Our bond with animals has strengthened more than ever. However, it is also true that some people find it more difficult than ever to keep pets. The number of families keeping pets has declined in Japan. The strong bond we have with pets and the declining ability to keep them seems contradictory, but are both brought about because of our deep love for them.

Post-reading activities: Individual

1

a Read paragraphs four and five again. What reasons does the author give for people keeping pets in their homes?

____

____

b Can you think of any other reasons why people keep pets nowadays?

____

____

c What's the most unusual pet you have ever seen or heard of? Why? Describe it.

____

____

Post-reading activities: Pairs/Small groups

d Share your answers from a, b, and c with a small group or new partner. Add any new information below.

____

____

____

____

2

a Keeping a pet is a big responsibility. With a partner or small group, choose a pet and write rules that you think people must follow to be responsible owners. Explain your answers whenever possible.

Rules for keeping a ____________________.

- **Example** *You must find a veterinarian close to your home and schedule regular checkups for your pet to make sure that it is in good health.*
-
-
-
-
-
-
-

b From the list above, circle your top three rules responsible pet owners must follow.

c Now share your top three rules with another pair or small group. After listening to everyone's answers, decide on a final set of three rules that you think responsible pet owners must follow. Write the answers below:

1. ____

   ____

2. ____

   ____

3. ____

   ____

Extension activities for
The Development of Relationships Between Humans and Animals

1 Find at least three people around you (friends or family) who have pets and interview them to understand why they keep pets. What are the positive points of keeping a pet? What are some difficult points about having a pet? Summarize your findings in at least seven sentences to share with your classmates.

OR

2 The article talks about good relationships between people and animals, but some people buy animals and then do not want them anymore. When this happens, sometimes people will release pets into the wild. Do some research into this issue. Why do people abandon pets today? What kind of pets are abandoned? What happens to abandoned pets, especially animals that are not common in Japan, such as racoons or capybaras? Summarize your findings in at least seven sentences to share with your classmates. Remember to cite your source.

Global Context

DL 13

You might not be surprised to hear that dogs are the most popular pets globally. But the most popular pet can actually differ depending on what country you live in. For example, while fish are globally in the top five most popular pets, they are number one in France. In Russia, over 50% of homes have at least one cat, making cats the most popular pet there. In Japan, the most popular pet is not cute or cuddly but is the long-horned beetle. Similarly, in China, while dogs are popular, many people also enjoy keeping crickets. And in nations like Australia and Brazil where cats and dogs are popular, many people also own birds. The kind of pet you keep can also be influenced by what is popular in your country.

Unit 7 Changing Forms of Celebrity in Japan

Activation activities: Pre-reading

a Who do you think were the earliest kind of celebrities (before television and magazines)? What did they do?

b Which do you prefer, celebrities who became famous from new media such as YouTube, or more traditional celebrities (movies, TV series, etc.)? Why?

c Would you want to be a celebrity? Why or why not?

d Share your answers from **a** – **c** with a small group or partner.

While-reading activities

a While reading the passage on the next page, list five words from the reading that you don't know. After you finish reading, check the meaning of each word. Finally, draw a picture of the word to help you remember it. Be prepared to share them with your classmates.

English word	Japanese meaning	A picture to help you remember the word	English word	Japanese meaning	A picture to help you remember the word
Example: entrepreneur	起業家		3.		
1.			4.		
2.			5.		

b In pairs or small groups, share your answers. Add any new words you learn from your classmates to the list below.

1.			3.		
2.			4.		

c What kind of celebrities were popular during each period? Find the information in the reading passage and write the examples in the chart below.

Time period	Kinds of celebrities
Edo period	
End of Edo period and Meiji period	
After Second World War	
Recently	

Reading

Changing Forms of Celebrity in Japan

Written by Kathryn M. Tanaka

DL 14

When you imagine a celebrity, what do you think of? A singer, an actor, a sports star, or perhaps an entrepreneur? Everyone's image of a celebrity is probably different. Who is treated as a celebrity and the kind of attention they receive can reflect a society's values and the way people engage with the media. Today, the kinds of media people use changes who is considered a celebrity and why.

In Japan the history of celebrity is long. Many experts say widely known celebrities in popular culture first appeared in the peaceful *Edo* period (1603-1868). This peace also brought changes in technology that made it easier to make and access printed materials. At the same time, *kabuki* theater, *sumo* wrestling, and the arts of the *geisha* also became widely popular. It is no surprise that Japan's earliest, well-known celebrities were *kabuki* actors, *sumo* wrestlers, and *geisha* whose images and art were celebrated in woodblock prints and books. Even when people could not see these stars in person, they enjoyed reading about them.

However, as technology changed, so did the nature of celebrity. Newspapers, photography, and film were introduced at the end of the *Edo* and early *Meiji* period (1868-1912). Authors such as Soseki Natsume (1867-1916) became famous by publishing their stories in newspapers. By the 1900s, there were magazines focused on film stars and other celebrities. These magazines also introduced a new kind of celebrity unique to Japanese cinema, the *benshi*, or voice actors who narrated early silent films.

After the Second World War, television again changed the nature of celebrity. The first widely watched television event in Japan was the wedding of the Japanese Crown Prince Akihito who married Michiko Shoda in 1959. After this event, television became an important part of popular culture. It led to the rise of a new wave of celebrities who performed on television in dramas, musical programs, variety shows, and comedies. Television also brought celebrities into peoples' homes for the first time.

More recently, technology has also changed the kinds of celebrities and how their fans interact with them. Social media platforms have allowed fans and celebrities to be closer than ever. SNS and YouTube allow anyone to share their ideas with a large audience at any time. Comment sections, short videos, and live streams promote interaction, and people can watch on their smartphones from anywhere, promoting relationships between media personalities and their fans. Japan, like most other countries in the world, has several YouTubers who are famous. They became so popular on YouTube that they became celebrities who now also write their own books or appear on TV and in magazines. With all of these changes over time, what kind of celebrities can we expect to see in the future?

Post-reading activities

1

a Select one celebrity from either the Edo, Meiji, Taisho, or Showa periods and describe them below. Why were they famous? Do you think they would be famous today? Why or why not?

____

____

____

b Share your findings with a partner. Does your partner agree with you about whether they would be famous today? Why or why not?

____

____

____

2

a What do you think are important characteristics and qualities of a celebrity? Think of examples together with your partner or group. Explain your answers.

Important Characteristics and Qualities of a Celebrity

- **Example** *likeable: many other people should like the person*
-
-
-
-
-
-
-
-

b Compare your answers with another group. Decide on the top three most important characteristics or qualities of a celebrity. Write the answers below:

1. ______________________________
2. ______________________________
3. ______________________________

3

a With your partner or in your group, think of three different kinds of celebrities. Write the name of the celebrity, the kind of celebrity they are, what they are famous for, and their characteristics and qualities. Be prepared to share your answers.

Time period	Kind of celebrities
Celebrity 1 Name:	
Kind of celebrity:	
Famous for:	
Qualities/Characteristics they are associated with	

Celebrity 2 Name:	
Kind of celebrity:	
Famous for:	
Qualities/Characteristics they are associated with	

Celebrity 3 Name:	
Kind of celebrity:	
Famous for:	
Qualities/Characteristics they are associated with	

b Take a class poll! Share your answers above with the class and vote on who is the most well-liked celebrity. Write the name of the celebrity below:

The most well-liked celebrity in this class is: ______________________________

Extension activities for Changing Forms of Celebrity in Japan

1 Pick a celebrity who was famous before 1990. What was their life like? What were they famous for? How did they become famous? Summarize your findings in at least seven sentences to share with your classmates. Remember to cite your source.

OR

2 Pick a country and research the most famous YouTube channel in that country. What kind of celebrity are they? Why are they popular? Watch some of their videos with English subtitles. Summarize your findings in at least seven sentences to share with your classmates. Remember to cite your source.

Global Context

DL 15

One of the things many people praise about YouTube is that anyone can access it, and anyone can make content. However, two popular YouTubers who might surprise you are Sally Parks and YuMi from North Korea. Although YouTube is blocked in North Korea, both channels have over a million subscribers and have gotten significant international media attention. Critics argue the channels are tightly controlled by the North Korean government and are used to spread the government's viewpoints. Despite these concerns, however, some people say that North Korean media should be freely available to people who want to research or view it. The interest and popularity of controversial channels can be both a strength and a problem for media like YouTube.

Unit 8

Popular Culture in Food

Activation activities: Pre-reading

a What is your favorite Japanese food? Why?

b • Here is a list of some seasonal flavors in Japan:

January to March: Strawberry
March to April: Cherry Blossom
May to June: Matcha (green tea)
June to July: Cherry
July to August: Watermelon
August to September: Peach
August to October: Grape, Pear
October to November: Sweet Potato, Chestnut, Pumpkin
December to January: Orange

• What are your favorite seasonal foods or drinks that use some of these flavors, or other seasonal flavors?

c What are some famous mascot characters (*yuru-kyara*) associated with food?

Example *Funassyi* is a cute pear character.

d Share your answers from a – c with a small group or partner.

While-reading activities

a While reading the passage on the next page, list five words from the reading that you don't know. After you finish reading, check the meaning of each word. Finally, find out the number of syllables for each word. Be prepared to share them with your classmates.

English word	Japanese meaning	Number of syllables
Example: seasonal	季節的	sea-son-al (3)
1.		
2.		
3.		
4.		
5.		

b In pairs or small groups, share your answers. Add any new words you learn from your classmates to the list below.

1.		
2.		
3.		

c According to the article, what are the three ways that pop culture meets food in Japan? Give an example of each.

The ways pop culture meets food in Japan	Examples
1.	
2.	
3.	

Popular Culture in Food

Written by Kathryn M. Tanaka

DL 16

When people think of Japanese food and popular culture, they often think of sushi. But in fact, this is too simple. Food and culture are connected in many different ways. Think of your daily life. Maybe while watching TV, you see a commercial for a new candy, or while riding the train, you see an advertisement for an energy drink, and the can has pictures from a popular anime character.

Food is a big popular culture business in Japan in several ways. Beginning in the 1990s, the television show *The Iron Chef* was shown around the world. People in many countries became familiar with Japanese food, and many began to eat it. Now, everyone knows what sushi is, along with other popular foods. After *washoku*, or Japanese food, was added to UNESCO's Intangible Cultural Heritage list, it became a global food.

However, many people would say *washoku* is not popular culture and anime-themed food packages are common all over the world. What else is unique about popular culture and food in Japan? Popular culture meets food in Japan in some very interesting ways. One way is through seasonal snack offerings. If you go to any convenience store in Japan, you will see "limited seasonal" flavors of food and drinks. These might include matcha, sweet potato, or strawberry. The flavors change often, and sometimes people are disappointed when they find a snack they like only to have it disappear.

Food is also a big part of local popular culture. If you ever travel in Japan, you will meet regional foods. For example, travelers to Osaka always make sure to eat *takoyaki*. You can also buy special, regional *takoyaki*-flavored snacks to take to your family or friends as souvenirs. More than characters, local flavors are a big part of both tourism culture and pop culture. Some local foods become so famous that they are made into *yuru-kyara* or characters that represent an area of Japan. For example, Mino City's mascot is *Takinomichi Yuzuru*, whose head is a yuzu fruit, and *Funassyi* from Chiba is a pear. *Funassyi* is now famous all over the world.

Finally, sometimes famous characters or meals from Japanese *anime* are sold as food in cafes or sometimes made into *kyaraben*, or character lunch boxes. There are even websites for fans of these "character *obento*" and children always seem very excited to eat them. Food that has appeared in *anime* is so popular that there are several cookbooks dedicated to making them. Thus, food is an important part of Japanese popular culture and although many people don't think about it, food and popular culture are important business in Japan.

Post-reading activities

1

a What are some specialty foods popular in different regions in Japan? Brainstorm as many as you can with a partner and write your ideas in the chart below.

Area in Japan	Specialty food	Description
Example: Osaka	takoyaki	Round balls of dough that have octopus in the middle and are covered with savory sauce.

b What is one of your favorite snacks or dishes from a foreign country? In your group, choose one snack or dish and describe it. Be ready to present it to the class.

Name of snack/dish and picture	Description

2

a Choose one of the following two activities and complete the task in the box below.

Activity 1 Find a seasonal food offering and write a review of it. Try to include an image of the food you sampled! Explain your design to your classmates.

OR

Activity 2 Design a new *yuru kyara* to promote a local food! Explain your design to your classmates.

Name: ______________________

Food: ______________________

Area: ______________________

Picture (Food / *yuru kyara*)

Description:

____

____

____

____

____

____

____

____

b Share your answers from **a** with another partner or small group.

Extension activities for Popular Culture in Food

1 Find an example of a food and pop culture media item in your daily life. It could be something such as a pop band with a convenience store deal or a cute character on a food item. Explain why this item is an example of a crossover of food and pop culture in Japan. Include an image, or bring the actual item to class. Summarize your findings in at least seven sentences to share with your classmates.

OR

2 Watch a TV show about food in Japan. What kinds of food do they introduce? How do they talk about it? How might a television show about food in Japan teach us about food and pop culture? Summarize your findings in at least seven sentences to share with your classmates. Remember to cite your source.

Global Context

DL 17

People have long been creative with food—sometimes dreaming up foods that do not exist. From movies to anime, food in fiction has long inspired real-world cuisine! One of the most famous examples is the broad selection of candy mentioned in the *Harry Potter* series including chocolate frogs, Bernie Bott's Every Flavor Beans, and Butter Beer. From fiction, these treats became reality, recreated in shops and theme parks for fans to try. Today, there are websites dedicated to fictional food that people try to make real, from the food mentioned in *Harry Potter* to snacks from *Alice in Wonderland*, and *Charlie and the Chocolate Factory*. If you love literature and are feeling creative, cuisine inspired by fiction is a tasty pop culture trend.

Unit 9 Cats and Their Powerful Influence on Japanese Culture

Activation activities: Pre-reading

a Have you ever been to a cat café? If yes, did you enjoy it? Explain why or why not. If not, do you want to go to one? Why or why not?

b Why do you think so many people love cats? Think of as many reasons as you can.

c What are some famous cats in Japan? Why are they famous?

d Share your answers from **a** – **c** with a small group or partner.

While-reading activities

a While reading the passage on the next page, list five words from the reading that you don't know. After you finish reading, check the meanings, and write an example sentence from a dictionary for each word so you can explain them to your classmates.

English word	Japanese meaning	Example sentence from the dictionary
Example: veterinarian	獣医	I take my dog to the veterinarian once a year for a checkup.
1.		
2.		
3.		
4.		
5.		

b In pairs or small groups, share your answers. Add any new words you learn from your classmates to the list below.

1.		
2.		
3.		

c The reading gives several examples of famous cats in Japan. Choose three examples from the reading and describe each one. Try to give more information about each cat.

Famous cat	Description	More information
1.		
2.		
3.		

Reading

Cats and Their Powerful Influence on Japanese Culture

Written by Kathryn M. Tanaka

DL 18

What is the most popular animal in Japan? Is it the *tsuru*, the crane, a symbol of long life and a popular design on *kimono* and other Japanese arts? Or could it be the *shiba-inu* or the *tanuki*? Some people might say the most popular and influential animal in Japan is the cat.

Cats are an important part of Japanese history, and they are important in popular culture today. Many people believe the first cats came to Japan during the Nara period (710-794), and have since become a big part of daily life. Cat stories are popular all over Japan, from monster cats (*bakeneko*) to cats that bring luck (*manekineko*). There are even some shrines for cats, such as *Nyannyanji* in Kyoto. Japan has also had cats working as train conductors, such as Wakayama's Tama-chan. Felines are also an important part of popular culture with Hello Kitty—although the creator has said the character is NOT a cat—being a well-known example. Many Japanese popular literature authors, such as Junichiro Tanizaki, Soseki Natsume, Haruki Murakami, and Sosuke Natsukawa have written fiction about cats. Felines appear in famous manga and anime, from Sailor Moon to Pokémon.

This love of cats in Japanese culture meant that they have often been kept as pets. However, living spaces became smaller when cities expanded, and buildings often banned pets. So, when the first cat cafe called *Mao Hoa Yuen* opened in Taipei in 1998, some entrepreneurs saw this as a way that could help Japanese people spend more time with cats. In 2004, a cafe called *Neko no Jikan* opened in Osaka. This started a boom in cat cafes across Japan. Such cafes allow people to relax and spend time with cats. The cafes may have different rules to keep the cats safe, such as limiting the number of visitors. However, even with rules and protections, there is a dark side. Some people argue it is hard to ensure the health of the animals, and not all cafes have access to care from veterinarians. Many cafes are small, and the animals may be kept in cages or tied up. What is seen as a fun and relaxing environment could be abusive to the animals.

Cats have played an important role in Japanese culture and many people enjoy spending time with them. However, we need to think seriously about their feelings and living conditions. The love, comfort, and enjoyment they bring should also be returned to the cats by giving them the best care. This includes not only in our homes, but also in places like cat cafes.

Post-reading activities

1

a Do you agree that cats are the most popular and important symbolic animal in Japan? Why or why not?

____

____

____

____

b What is another important animal in Japanese culture? Describe it and explain why it is important. Compare answers with a partner. Do you agree with their answers? Why or why not?

____

____

____

____

c Share your answers from 1 a – b with a small group or partner.

2

a In a group, list all of the pros and cons of cat cafes.

Pros
Cons

b Make an argument supporting the side you agree with. Share it with your group.

____

____

c Which person in your group do you think has the best argument? Why?

____

____

3 Imagine that you and your partner or group are part of a cat activist group. You want to create new laws to protect cats. Think of at least three new laws and describe them in detail. Draw a symbol to represent each new law. When you are finished, share your laws with the class.

Symbol	Law & Description
1.	
2.	
3.	

Extension activities for
Cats and Their Powerful Influence on Japanese Culture

1. Pick a country and research an important symbolic animal there. What are some traditions or stories associated with the animal? How is the animal a part of that country's culture today? Summarize your findings in at least seven sentences to share with your classmates. Remember to cite your source.

OR

2. Disagree with the reading. Pick a different animal and find research to support the idea that the cat is not the most important animal in Japan, but your animal of choice is. Summarize your findings and ideas in at least seven sentences to share with your classmates. Remember to cite your source.

Global Context

DL 19

Cats are not only famous in Japan. Cats have inspired movies like *Cats* and *Garfield*. Cats are in some of the most beloved children's books written in English, such as *The Cat in the Hat* by Dr. Seuss. They appear in fairy tales as well as films based on fairy tales such as *Puss in Boots*. Within the *Looney Tunes* cartoon universe, the cat Sylvester continuously chases Tweety Bird, and Tom is also always unsuccessfully chasing Jerry. Even Disney has made beloved films about cats such as the 1970 animated film *The Aristocats*, and the 1988 retelling of Charles Dickens' *Oliver Twist*, *Oliver & Company*, which casts Oliver the Cat as an important character. Cats are not only symbolic in different cultures and useful to people, but in pop culture, they provide important entertainment too.

Unit 10

Language and Japanese Media

Activation activities: Pre-reading

a What do you think are some of the most difficult parts of learning a foreign language such as English? Why?

b What do you think could be some of the most difficult parts of learning Japanese as a foreign language? Why?

c How do you think parts of your identity are reflected in language? Explain your answer in at least two sentences.

d Share your answers from a – c with a small group or partner.

While-reading activities

a While reading the passage on the next page, list five words from the reading that you don't know. After you finish reading, check the meanings, and write an example sentence from a dictionary for each word so you can explain them to your classmates.

English word	Japanese meaning	Example sentence from the dictionary
Example: dialect	方言	He spoke the local dialect, so I could not understand him.
1.		
2.		
3.		
4.		
5.		

b In pairs or small groups, share your answers. Add any new words you learn from your classmates to the list below.

1.		
2.		
3.		

c Write a short, one-sentence summary: What is each paragraph in the article about?

1. Language tells us many things about a person and is also connected to pop culture.
2. ______________________________
3. ______________________________
4. ______________________________
5. ______________________________

Language and Japanese Media

Written by Kathryn M. Tanaka

DL 20

Spoken language is important because it communicates more than just what we say. It can give important hints about gender, social class, age, or even where a person is from. Language is connected to popular culture in ways we don't often think about. For example, in things like movies, anime, and video games, language becomes very important. In stories, language helps create a character because it reflects a person's personality. However, this can create challenges too.

There are a lot of stereotypes associated with language in Japan. Think about what you imagine when you think of *Kansai-ben* or the Kansai area dialect. What do you think of when you hear the word *joseigo* or female language? What about *keigo* or honorific language? What about slang or curse words? For many Japanese people, these elements of language are a part of daily life that people don't think about, but in fact, they carry a lot of stereotypes and assumptions about the people who use those kinds of language.

Linguistic Professor Peter Backhaus says that language has become an issue in the translation of manga, books, and subtitles for films and anime. He says that in many kinds of movies or stories, Japanese uses what Professor Satoshi Kinsui calls *yakuwarigo*, or role language, to create an image of a stereotypical kind of character. Therefore, characters playing policemen in anime might speak one way while a *yakuza* member has very different speech patterns. Kansai dialect might be used to highlight the fact that a character is funny.

Joseigo, or female language, is slightly different from the two examples above. Women often use different first-person pronouns than men and often avoid rough second-person pronouns like *omae*. Women also might use different language at the end of their sentences, such as *kashira*. Moreover, women use *keigo* or honorific language more often than men, which some scholars say has the effect of making women seem passive. In media, *joseigo* can be used to highlight feminine characters.

Role language can be difficult to translate back into Japanese, too. If other countries do not have a system of *keigo*, should Japanese translators use *keigo* when translating a conversation between a company boss and a new employee? If they are writing movie subtitles for a tough policewoman, should they use very feminine *joseigo*? If a politician uses curse words or incorrect grammar, should translators also make mistakes and use rough language? There are no easy answers to these questions, but there are many ways in which *yakuwarigo* is a part of media and it can create stereotypes. This means it is important to think about language and bias in the media around us.

Post-reading activities: Individual

a Write down three open-ended discussion questions you can ask after reading the article.

1. ______________________________
2. ______________________________
3. ______________________________

Examples of open-ended discussion questions:
Why do you think...? How do you feel about...? Would you rather ... or ...? If you were..., what would you do? Have you ever...? What do you think is the best way to...?

b Write your answers to your three open-ended discussion questions above.

1. ______________________________
2. ______________________________
3. ______________________________

Post-reading activities: In pairs or a small group

1

a Ask a classmate your three discussion questions and write their answers in the table below.

b Do you agree or disagree with their opinion? Why? Explain to your partner why you agree or disagree.

a Name: Classmate 1's answers:	**b** Do you agree or disagree with their opinion? Why? I (dis) agree because...
1.	
2.	
3.	

2

a In what other ways do you think identity is expressed in language? List more examples that are not mentioned in the reading for both Japanese and English.

Japanese	English

b Listen to another pair or small group's list and add new points in the table below.

Japanese	English

Post-reading activities

3

a After reading the article and completing the exercises, how would you revise or expand your answer to the question "How do you think parts of your identity are reflected in language?" This question was first asked in 1 c on page 60. Give specific examples.

b Share your answers from 3 a a with a small group or partner.

Extension activities for Language and Japanese Media

1 The article gives the example of the Kansai dialect, but there are many different dialects around Japan. Pick a different dialect and research it. What are some special features of the dialect? How does the language relate to identity? Summarize your findings in at least seven sentences to share with your classmates. Remember to cite your source.

OR

2 The article discusses how age, gender, social class, region, and other things are reflected in language. Pick one of these things and do some further research on it. What are some special features of the language? How does it relate to identity? Summarize your findings in at least seven sentences to share with your classmates. Remember to cite your source.

Global Context

DL 21

For many people, the hardest language in the world to learn is not Japanese or English. According to UNESCO, it's Mandarin. There are several reasons for this, but one of them is the fact that Mandarin is not phonetic, which means the characters used in written Chinese give you no clue about how to pronounce them. To read Chinese, people need to learn thousands of different characters. Other languages have challenges though, as well. Hungarian and Finnish, for example, have very difficult grammar rules that can be hard to master. Using the wrong intonation in languages like Thai or Vietnamese can completely change the meaning of a word. Depending on what your skills are, it may be easier for you to learn some languages and more difficult to learn others.

Unit 11

Human Rights and Japanese Pop Culture

Activation activities: Pre-reading

a | What is your favorite manga? Why?

b | What are some current human rights issues in Japan?

c | Give an example of a manga which deals with a human rights issue. What is the issue it addresses?

d | Share your answers from a – c with a small group or partner.

While-reading activities

a While reading the passage on the next page, list five words from the reading that you don't know. After you finish reading, check the meaning of each word. Finally, create a word scramble for your words. Start the scramble with the first letter of the word and be sure to capitalize it. Be prepared to share them with your classmates.

English word	Japanese meaning	Word scramble
Example: Human trafficking	人身売買	Hmuna Tfickfragni
1.		
2.		
3.		
4.		
5.		

b Cover your five English words and exchange books with a partner. Looking at the Japanese meanings and word scrambles of your partner's five words, how many of them can you unscramble in three minutes?

Partner's Unscramble:		
Example: 人身売買	Hmuna Tfickfragni:	Human Trafficking
1.		
2.		
3.		
4.		
5.		

c The reading gives nine examples of manga which are centered on human rights issues. Complete the table below by writing the names of five manga and the human rights that each one addresses.

Name of the Manga	Human Rights Issue
1.	
2.	
3.	
4.	
5.	

Reading

Human Rights and Japanese Pop Culture

Written by Kathryn M. Tanaka

DL 22

What is a human right? Do you know what your human rights are? Are they important in your daily life? Many people enjoy their human rights without thinking about them. But access to human rights changes depending on where you live, how old you are, your gender, your sexuality, and many other things. In practice, not everyone has the same human rights. But many people think that human rights violations are only a problem in other countries, not in Japan. In fact, there are human rights problems in Japan as well.

Gender identity and sexual orientation disorder, poverty, discrimination, justice, human trafficking, depression, and physical abuse are just a few of the human rights problems in Japan. And all of these subjects are topics in popular culture, in particular in manga and anime. This is important because manga and anime are popular all over the world, and are accessible to many different readers from children to adults, so the way human rights are represented becomes very important.

What are some human rights issues in manga you might have enjoyed? For example, *Otouto no Otto* (My Brother's Husband) is about a Canadian man who marries a Japanese man and goes to stay with the Japanese husband's brother and niece after the death of his Japanese husband. *IS* (short for Intersex) deals with intersex individuals and the challenges they face in Japanese society. Other manga such as *NieA_7* or *Dai-Tokyo Binbō Seikatsu Manual* ("Greater Tokyo Poverty Living Manual") highlight the issue of poverty.

Children's human rights are also important. *Hikari to Tomo ni* (With the Light) focuses on a family raising an autistic son and his challenges to communicate, whereas *Chiisai Hito* (Little People) features a child welfare caseworker and a survivor of child abuse who is working to improve the lives of troubled children. We can also find manga that talks about disability, illness, or confinement. *Real* features wheelchair basketball players. More recently, *Mugi Baa no Shima* (Grandma Mugi's Island) addresses the problem of Hansen's disease in Japan, and *Mori no Asagao* (Morning Glories of the Forest) shows life on death row in Japan as well as raising victims' rights issues.

All of these manga demonstrate how human rights issues are connected. For example, questions about family, nation, and relationships are all dealt with in *Otouto no Otto*. *Mugi Baa no Shima* focuses on health discrimination but also raises issues of women's rights, motherhood, and fertility. Manga helps readers understand how human rights issues intersect even if the focus is on one main issue.

Manga and anime are popular all over the world, not only in Japan. When human rights issues are represented in manga, it becomes easier for people to talk about them. Moreover, social change becomes possible once people begin to talk and debate what human rights are and how they should be protected. Manga is an important tool to help make this happen.

Image from *Mugi Baa no Shima* by Furubayashi Kaigetsu

Post-reading activities

1

a Choose one country and conduct an internet search to find out three current human rights issues that the country is facing. Complete the following table by listing the human rights issues and a short description of each of them.

Country: ______________________________

Human Rights Issue	A Description of the Issue
Example: Power Harassment	In June of this year, the government made a set of rules in which all businesses must follow to prevent power harassment in the workplace.
1.	
2.	
3.	

b Interview two of your classmates to find out about the human rights issues in the countries they selected. Complete the table below by listing two human rights issues and a short description of them.

Partner 1's Name: _________________________ **Country:** _________________________

Human Rights Issue	A Description of the Issue
1.	
2.	

Partner 2's Name: _________________________ **Country:** _________________________

Human Rights Issue	A Description of the Issue
1.	
2.	

2

a With a partner design a poster to help raise awareness of one human rights violation in Japan.

b Listen to two poster presentations. While listening to each poster presentation, write what you learned from it and one question you have about it. At the end of each poster presentation, ask your question and write the presenter's answer.

Names:	What did you learn?	Question & Answer
	Human Rights Issue: **Description of the Problem:**	**Q:** **A:**
Names:	**What did you learn?**	**Question & Answer**
	Human Rights Issue: **Description of the Problem:**	**Q:** **A:**

c Which poster was the most interesting for you? Why? Write complete sentences giving at least two reasons:

Extension activities for Human Rights and Japanese Pop Culture

1. Pick a manga mentioned in the article or find an example of your own. Describe the manga and discuss how it depicts human rights issues. What does it talk about? Why is it important? Summarize your findings in at least seven sentences to share with your classmates. Remember to cite your source.

OR

2. Research a human rights issue in Japan. What is it? Who is affected? What is being done to help the issue? Why is it still a problem? Summarize your findings in at least seven sentences to share with your classmates. Remember to cite your source.

Global Context

DL 23

Many people say that comic books are not manga. But comic books and manga both use pictures and words to tell stories in creative new ways. Like manga, comic books also take up issues of human rights. For example, *Citizen 13660* (1946) and *They Called Us the Enemy* (2019) tell the stories of the authors' experiences of being kept in American prison camps for citizens with a Japanese background during World War II. *Persepolis* (2003) describes the author's childhood and early adult years in Iran during the Islamic Revolution. *Climate Changed: A Personal Journey through the Science* (2014) discusses climate crises through history, science, and personal narrative. There are graphic novels and manga around the world highlighting social justice and human rights issues—how many can you find to read?

Unit 12

Cuteness

Activation activities: Pre-reading

a | What does the word cute mean to you? You can use a dictionary to help you if necessary.

b | Give three examples of how businesses use "cute" in advertising.

c | What are some different types of cuteness or "*kawaii*"? Describe what they are.

e.g., *kimo-kawaii* – Gross/cute

d | Share your answers from a – c with a small group or partner.

While-reading activities

a While reading the passage on the next page, list five words from the reading that you don't know. After you finish reading, check the meaning of each word. Finally, make a word search with the five words in the graph below. Be prepared to share it with your classmates.

English word	Japanese meaning
Example: Fantasy	ファンタジー

Example Word Search (Find the word *Fantasy*.) Now make your own word search using five words from the *Cuteness* article.

T	F	B	S	U	Y	C	I	F	X	F	Y
N	Y	A	T	V	H	T	R	S	B	A	E
J	Z	R	N	Y	A	G	T	Y	F	N	T
P	F	A	S	T	F	N	G	H	F	S	W
W	S	C	F	V	A	N	T	S	S	A	N
K	E	Q	B	V	R	S	F	A	T	G	A
N	F	P	V	T	S	S	Y	E	Z	Y	F

Your Words: 1. ____________ ____________ 2. ____________ ____________

3. ____________ ____________ 4. ____________ ____________

5. ____________ ____________

Your Word Search

b Exchange textbooks with a partner. How many of their words can you find in two minutes?

c The reading uses several nouns (*meishi*) and adjectives (*keiyoushi*) to describe cuteness. While reading, write these words in the box below. Indicate if the word is a noun (n) or adjective (adj). Be sure to use a dictionary to check the meanings of any new words.

Example sweetness (n); soft (adj.)

Reading

Cuteness

Written by Lorraine Plourde[2]

DL 24

かわいい

Cuteness is a cultural form which many people have argued is deeply connected to shopping, advertising, and the female gender. It has been defined in terms of sweetness, delicateness, and weakness. Additionally, cuteness can be associated with children. Features that are often associated with cuteness include a round face, big eyes, and a large head. More importantly, these marks of cuteness help create images of helplessness or weakness. In other words, there is a link between cute objects and the feelings they generate, such as weakness and helplessness.

Cuteness is described as *kawaii* in Japanese. In many ways, the Japanese concept of *kawaii* is much like the English term for cute as they are both presented as sweet, delicate, and innocent. Moreover, *kawaii* is rooted in the Japanese term for pitiful or pathetic (*kawaiso*), adding another layer of weakness.

Kawaii is a concept that became popular in the 1960s as it became widely used in everyday language and advertising. *Kawaii* culture emerged after the war when Japan's economy was growing and becoming stronger in the 1970s, and women were gaining more freedom to consume products. First associated with young women, cute culture grew during the 1970s and 1980s. By the mid-1990s, large companies used *kawaii* culture which soon spread to goods, roadwork signs, and delivery trucks.

Some people argue that cute cultural forms such as cute objects and fashion are a way for young women to reject the responsibilities of being adults. *Kawaii* culture has been seen as a kind of resistance to everyday life in Japan. Because *kawaii* is connected with young women, cuteness can be a way to get away from "male" rules and control. Cuteness is also connected to shopping, leisure, play, and fantasy, but it is rooted in everyday life. Cute is a part of work, labor, and reality. While they seem very different, they can sometimes exist together, such as in the case of cute uniforms (leisure, play, and fantasy) at private schools (work and reality).

Cuteness can also be viewed as a form of soft power in the "Cool Japan" image branding promoted by the Japanese government. "*Kawaii*" began in Japanese popular culture before it was an economic and political tool, but "Cool Japan" is now used as a form of nation branding or soft power to increase Japanese influence around the world. Both "cute" and "cool" are always being changed to serve new purposes, such as companies or businesses wanting to make money. Ideas about "cool" and "cute" are used in different ways by the government, businesses, and people themselves. When we think about what is "cool" and what is "cute," we also need to think about why the concept is being used. We must think about the history and the political meaning the terms sometimes have.

[2] Adapted from *Japanese Media and Popular Culture: An Open-Access Digital Initiative of the University of Tokyo* published 18 April 2020. Available online: https://jmpc-utokyo.com/keyword/cuteness/

Post-reading activities

1

a Choose three people or things which you consider to be cute. Complete the following table by listing the type of cuteness and a short description of why you think each of them is cute.

Example	Type of Cuteness	What is unusual about this kind of cute?
Sento-kun (Nara city mascot)	*Kimo-Kawaii*	He is very strange. He is not cute, but he is weird and that makes him cute.
1.		
2.		
3.		

b Interview three of your classmates and add two of their answers in the tables below.

Partner 1's Name: ______________________________

Person or Thing	Type of Cuteness	Why are they considered cute?
1.		
2.		

Partner 2's Name: ______________________________ **Country:** ______________________________

Person or Thing	Type of Cuteness	Why are they considered cute?
1.		
2.		

Partner 3's Name: ______________________________ **Country:** ______________________________

Person or Thing	Type of Cuteness	Why are they considered cute?
1.		
2.		

2

a Do you think cute is important to Japan's image abroad? Why or why not?

b In a small group discuss your answers from **2** **a**. Add any new points below.

c You are responsible for designing a cute product for your company. Choose an item from the box below and design a cute advertisement for it. Explain your design.

washing machine / wrist watch / car / wheelchair / a can for a softdrink

Explanation

Picture

d Share your answer from **c** with a small group or partner.

Extension activities for Cuteness

1 There are many kinds of cute subcultures in Japan today, such as *yumekawaii*, *kimokawaii*, or *gurokawaii*. Pick a cute subculture and find an example of a picture or good that represents that cute subculture. What features does it share with *kawaii* discussed in the article? What are some unusual or new features in the cute subculture you researched? Summarize your findings in at least seven sentences to share with your classmates. Remember to cite your source.

OR

2 The article mentions "Cool Japan." Do some research, and share your ideas. What exactly is it? When did it start? What characters are associated with it? How is it different from Cute Japan? How is Cool Japan used in business or politics? Summarize your findings in at least seven sentences to share with your classmates. Remember to cite your source.

Global Context

DL 25

Every culture in the world has some appreciation for what we might consider "cute," as associated with attractiveness, and often youthfulness and femininity. In South Korea, people might say *aegyo*, and in China perhaps *ke'ai*, both of which express ideas similar to the Japanese idea of *kawaii*. In Thailand, the word *sanook* expresses something cute, but also fun and cheerful. The German word *süß* and the Polish word *słodki* can mean sweet and cute and are used with babies and animals more likely to be regarded as "cute." Finally, a country like Jamaica might have a broader idea of what cute can be. In Jamaica, words that have similar meanings to "cute" can be used to describe people no matter what their age, ethnicity, or body type is. So, while "kawaii" might be a global aesthetic, ideas about what is "cute" can change from culture to culture.

Active Listening Worksheets (Photocopiable)

Directions: You will listen to several reports today. Choose three of them. While listening, write two things that you learned and one question you have for the presenter. At the end of the report, ask your question and write the presenter's answer. Finally, write your opinion. At the end of class, choose one report that you found to be the most interesting, and write about it below.

Presenter 1	**Title:**	**Question and Answer**
Name:	Two things you learned: Your opinion:	Q: A:

Presenter 2	**Title:**	**Question and Answer**
Name:	Two things you learned: Your opinion:	Q: A:

Presenter 3	**Title:**	**Question and Answer**
Name:	Two things you learned: Your opinion:	Q: A:

Which report was the most interesting for you? Why? Write complete sentences and give at least two reasons:

____

____

____

Contributing Authors' Biographies

Rossella Ceccarini holds a PhD in Global Studies from Sophia University, Tokyo. Her doctoral research, and following publications, focused on the development of Italian cuisine in Japan. She is currently based in Ireland, working in the field of corporate learning and development. While looking at ways to train and engage adult learners in their work environment, she keeps a vivid interest in Japan and food culture.

Yoshimi Kurata is a manga artist, a member of the Japan Manga Association, and a professor at Otemae University. Among his many works, Kurata may be best known for his Aji Ichi Monme series, which began in 1984 and now spans over 70 volumes while it is still being serialized in magazines. It has been adapted into a TV drama and earned him the 44th Shogakukan Manga Award in 1999. Kurata also serves as a judge in global manga competitions and conducts workshops around the world.

Yuka Nakajima is an Associate Professor of Psychology at Otemae University. Her research focuses on the psychological benefits of human-animal interaction. Specifically, she investigates the ways in which animals can help individuals cope with stress and achieve their goals.

Lorraine Plourde is an Associate Professor of Anthropology and Media Studies and Chair of the Anthropology Department at SUNY Purchase. Her research focuses on sound and listening in contemporary Japan with a particular focus on sensory ethnography, examining how people's moods are effectively targeted through public spaces such as classical music cafes, department stores, and cat cafes. Her newer research projects include cuteness and girlhood studies (specifically the Japanese pop-metal group Babymetal) and children's music and surrealism.

Mark Schiller is a reporter, critic, and author specializing in Japanese films and popular culture. He has been a regular film critic at *The Japan Times*, Japan's oldest and largest English-language newspaper, since 1989. He has covered the Japanese film industry for "Screen International" from 1990 to 2005 and for "Variety" from 2005 to the present. He has also published multiple books covering Japanese popular culture, film, and fiction. He has consulted on many films and was the author of the award-winning film "Convenience Story" (2022).

Carmen Săpunaru Tămaș is currently the coordinator of the Japanese language and culture program at the University of Hyogo. After obtaining her PhD from Osaka University in 2009, she has been teaching Japanese mythology and anthropology at Osaka University, Kobe University, and Doshisha University. Her most recent publications include: "Beliefs, Ritual Practices and Celebrations in Kansai" (Pro Universitaria 2019, 2022, 2023), and "Forms of the Body in Contemporary Japanese Society, Literature, and Culture" (edited with Irina Holca, Lexington Books 2020).

Textbook Authors' Biographies

Robert Sheridan (M.S.Ed. in TESOL) is an associate professor in the Faculty of Agriculture at Kindai University in Nara, Japan. After earning his teaching certification in his home country of Canada, he moved to Japan where he has taught for over 20 years in primary, secondary, and post-secondary institutions. His research interests and publications include topics related to vocabulary acquisition, CLIL, extensive reading, student-centered learning, and culture in education.

Kathryn M. Tanaka (PhD) is an associate professor at the University of Hyogo. Her work focuses on literature and culture in language education, and connects these fields to global issues in her pedagogy and research. She has published in a variety of areas, including Japanese literature and culture, and human rights in language education.

Jeanette M. Kobayashi (M.Sc.Ed.) is an assistant professor at Doshisha Women's College of Liberal Arts. Her interests are rooted in constructivism and educational psychology, and she continuously works to help create the best learning environments and materials for second language acquisition.

MEMO

著作権法上、無断複写・複製は禁じられています。

Japanese Popular Culture in English: Discussions and Critical Thinking ［B-964］
日本のポップカルチャーで学ぶディスカッションと批判的思考

1 刷　2024 年 2 月 26 日

著　者　Robert Sheridan　シェリダン・ロバート
Kathryn M. Tanaka　田中　キャサリン
Jeanette M. Kobayashi　小林　ジネマリー

発行者　南雲　一範　Kazunori Nagumo
発行所　株式会社　南雲堂
〒162-0801　東京都新宿区山吹町361
NAN'UN-DO Co., Ltd.
361 Yamabuki-cho, Shinjuku-ku, Tokyo 162-0801, Japan
振替口座 : 00160-0-46863
TEL:　03-3268-2311（営業部:学校関係）
03-3268-2384（営業部:書店関係）
03-3268-2387（編集部）
FAX:　03-3269-2486

編集者　中西　史子

組　版　柴崎　利恵

装　丁　奥定　泰之

装　画　大河原　波子

検　印　省　略

コード　ISBN978-4-523-17964-1　C0082

Printed in Japan

E-mail : nanundo@post.email.ne.jp
URL : https://www.nanun-do.co.jp/